What I
FOUND
When I Wasn't Looking

A BOOK OF PICTURES, POETRY AND PROSE

SHARON J. MILLICAN

WestBow Press books may be ordered through booksellers or by contacting:

WestBow Press
A Division of Thomas Nelson & Zondervan
1663 Liberty Drive
Bloomington, IN 47403
www.westbowpress.com
844-714-3454

Because of the dynamic nature of the Internet, any web addresses or links contained in this book may have changed since publication and may no longer be valid. The views expressed in this work are solely those of the author and do not necessarily reflect the views of the publisher, and the publisher hereby disclaims any responsibility for them.

ISBN: 979-8-3850-3251-8 (sc)
ISBN: 979-8-3850-3252-5 (e)

Library of Congress Control Number: 2024918295

Print information available on the last page.

WestBow Press rev. date: 10/22/2024

WESTBOW
PRESS®
A DIVISION OF THOMAS NELSON
& ZONDERVAN

This book is dedicated to Mama who inspired my first
published poem (The Light Beyond the Shadows)

(Thank you to all family and friends) You are a daily inspiration

Thanks Tamarah, for letting Parker, Troubles, Waylon & Jessi
be a part of: What I Found When I Wasn't Looking

Thanks Angie and Charlie, for Number 88 and her calf

Thanks to Larry Millican, for yet, another author picture!

What I Found When I Wasn't Looking

I lived in the valley
My little world, quite content
The solitude that surrounded me
I viewed as Heaven sent

The violence and nightmares
Had been put to rest
According to (Me)
My life was the best

There were cool creeks
To play in
And fresh air
I could breathe
If my life could be better
I couldn't believe

One day I decided,
I couldn't say why
To climb that high mountain
And see the other side

I climbed that high mountain
I saw blue skies above
And when I wasn't looking
It was then, I found love

Mr. Hummingbird

Mr. ruby-throated hummingbird
Come let me watch you fly
I will gladly give you nectar
As you quickly dart by

Look me in the eye
Buzz around my ear
I'll watch for you consistently
Each and every year

I'll plant some pretty flowers
That should be a healthy snack
Then gaze at you for hours
While the flutter of your wings
Move you forward
Then move you back

Don't forget me Mr. Hummingbird
You are a gift - you are a treasure
I'll see you in the spring
Because you are my pleasure

Easter Lilies to Me

Some call them Jonquils
Others say daffodils
I call them Easter Lilies
When I see them in the fields

You know, those yellow flowers,
In early spring, they grow
Sometimes their beauty can be seen
In a late winter snow

When I see them every year,
I remember when I was a child
The happiness, in my mama's voice,
So sweet, and soft, and mild

As the morning sun filtered through
My windowpane so bright
It shone across her auburn hair
And her jade green eyes
"I still yet see the light"

Just one more precious gift
A childhood memory
Tells why that springtime flower is an
Easter Lily to me

When the Storm Comes In

She watched with the greatest of calm
As dark clouds came rolling by
Threatening to invade the peace and
beauty of her clear, blue sky

The woman seemed so placid, so unaware
Was there not a thought
of the danger lurking there?

But then there came a glimpse
In her faded blue eyes
A strength I had not seen before
She was tranquil, strong and wise

As I watched the able woman
I finally realized
She had weathered many storms
In the seasons that had passed her by

She holds my admiration
For the woman she's always been
I have no doubt she will survive
When the storm comes in

Raindrops and Sunshine

Her pace was quick
She held her head high
But her young face told a story
as the world passed her by
She was walking down a lonely road
And she carried a mighty heavy load

The clouds blew in and the raindrops fell
She was getting weaker, I could tell
Someone stopped her on that stormy day
To help the girl on her weary way

Unless the raindrops come my Dear
They say a rainbow cannot appear
When the sun comes out and the raindrops glow
The heavens could hold your next rainbow

Little Hijacker

So timid you appear
You are a small bit shy
Tilt your pretty head
As if to ask me why
I do the things I do
I love you Little Guy

When I am all alone
My world empty and still
You fill my cup and suddenly
Change the way I feel

You look so very innocent
Pretend that you're not smart
But you're just a little hijacker
A stealer of my heart

Troubles

Troubles was born one of a kind
That's where she got her name
She was always into something
And rightfully took the blame

If a fence came down
There she was tangled in the wire
If the creek was up
You could bet Troubles was
"Singing in the choir"

Yes, Trouble she was
As she ran amuck
With the other calves and cows
She was wild as a buck
And if she was to stay
Nobody knew just how

Well, the years passed fast
Troubles, the calf, didn't last
She soon had a calf of her own
She was all settled down
Ready to work
Best cow on the farm
Troubles was finally grown

The Squirrel and the Blue Jay

The day was warm; and bright was the sun
I couldn't wait to get out and join the fun

I loved the spring in all its new-birth
It made me feel healthy, down to earth

I sat quiet and still, to watch the creatures pass by
It wasn't too long- I saw the Blue Jay fly

There was so much beauty in those outstretched wings
Such peace and contentment, springtime brings

Well in a split second, I lost that sweet calm
When with vicious intent, she did a dive-bomb

The sweet little squirrel ran fast, she was free
She found her sweet shelter in a nearby tree

I watched for a week, till I figured it out
Now I don't want to judge, there is no doubt

The squirrel and the Blue Jay are meant to live free
And the best I can do is to let nature be

The Squirrel and the Blue Jay

. . . .

(Thou Shalt Not Judge)

Raven, my German Shepherd, woke me from a deep sleep when she dropped her chin on the edge of my bed. That was her subtle way of telling me it was time to start our day. I rolled out of the bed and took a quick shower. I pulled on my jeans and a sweat shirt. The early spring day was still yet cool. I grabbed my camera, on the run, slipped my cold feet into my tennis shoes and we headed outside. While taking a short walk, I could hear the birds chirping in the wooded area just beyond my backyard.

Eventually, we settled on the back porch. I had a mug of hot chocolate. My camera, as usual, was nearby. It wasn't long until a Blue Jay appeared. She came close enough to stir that nature feeling. Her blue and silver wings had a translucent glow in the early morning sunlight. She was pretty magnificent.

Well, that tender, calm feeling didn't last long. Suddenly, a cute little squirrel was in sight and that savage little Blue Jay was diving at her, ferociously. She flicked her fluffy tail and lit out for the nearest branch. It took her to what seemed a safe distance away from that pesky old Blue Jay.

Several times a day, I made it a point to go out and observe that bit of nature. I wanted to see just how mean Blue Jays really are. I had no idea. I was a bit shocked at myself for being so angry with the Blue Jay. After the first couple of days, I looked a little more closely and a short distance into the bushes and trees, I could see the squirrel's path was to a tall tree with a large nest in it. I knew, then that the poor little squirrel, most likely had a nest of babies up there.

Well then, I was really developing next to hatred for that mean, old Blue Jay! I got to thinking, "I'll bet that Blue Jay is after that nest of baby squirrels! I did my research and sure enough; Blue Jays are known to feast on newborn baby squirrels! The information did not help my feelings of dislike for the Blue Jay!

I continued to watch, off and on, all week. It dawned on me that I had never seen the Blue Jay fly near the squirrel's nest. That struck me as very odd. I realized the squirrel was in the same area every time the Blue Jay did her little dive-bomb! That area was several yards from the squirrel's nest.

By this time, I was becoming a little confused as to what was really going on in this relationship between the Blue Jay and the squirrel. They were both so persistent and consistent in the way they were handling their daily activities. Then, it dawned on me; "I'll bet that Blue Jay has a nest of eggs out there!" Well, sure enough, when I saw that sweet little Blue Jay sitting in her nest, protecting her eggs, my hateful feelings for her quickly dwindled away. Those feelings were replaced with a feeling of admiration.

I did my research, once more, and found that squirrels are notorious for eating eggs. Now, I could have assumed that the squirrel was causing all the trouble and was after the Blue Jay's eggs, making the bird totally innocent and the squirrel a vicious, little rodent. Not a chance! I was not letting myself fall into that trap again!

(The fact is that during my week of observing nature, I developed a far greater respect for what is called, the wild!)
Maybe, they had no mutual feelings of hate, or even dislike for the other. Maybe, they were just, simply, protecting their young.

The Pear Tree

Have you ever felt useless
ragged and worn
All frazzled, not pretty,
Unhappy, forlorn?

Let me tell you a story
And you might see
That you are just as
Beautiful as my old pear tree

A few weeks ago
I almost cut her down
Some of her beautiful limbs broke
And had fallen to the ground

Soon after, a summer storm came
The wind blew hard
Stripped some more limbs off
And threw them in the yard

Big pears were scattered everywhere
What a mess that pear tree made
Without strong branches or her pretty leaves
She could no longer offer shade

I stood back and compared the ugly tree
To the beauty of all the rest
Then just before, I cut her down
I realized, my used up broken tree
Without a doubt, is the very best

The Pear Tree

· ·

A few short years ago, I bought a small pear tree for my yard. I searched for just the right place to do the planting. Deciding it would be best suited, not too far from a larger fruitless pear and a pretty maple tree; I dug the hole. The pear tree grew fast and strong. A couple of years later, I planted an apple tree on the opposite side of the pear tree. By the time I saw pears, all four trees were making a nice, shaded area in my yard. And, the spring season brought beautiful blossoms from the fruit trees.

Well, by the spring of 2,024, that pear tree stood tall and was a gorgeous sight to see. The limbs stretched out and were covered with thick, healthy leaves. I wondered if there would be much of a pear crop in 2024. Time answered that question and the answer was, yes.

When the pretty blossoms fell off and the tiny buds came and went, it wasn't long until that pear tree was swaying beneath its many luscious pears. And the pears kept coming and growing larger and larger. Then one night, the pear tree began to break under the pressure. It had become so productive, that while I was sleeping, the tree broke under its heavy load. I awoke to several broken limbs.

After a couple of weeks, a strong windstorm came. The pear tree was hit and, again, limbs came crashing down. Large, unripe pears were scattered over the ground. The beautiful, strong, productive pear tree looked useless, ragged and worn. It had lost so many limbs and almost all the fruit it had carried. Its beauty had faded. The tree appeared to be, near worthless. In fact, it was so stripped of limbs and leaves, the tree could no longer offer, as much as a small shade.

Well, there soon came a time, a decision had to be made. What should we do with that lopsided, broken pear tree? To even it up, so many branches would have to be cut, that it would be about the size of a small bush. It would have no pears, no shade, no pretty branches and not many leaves.

I almost said, "Just cut it down!" But, as we continued to pick up the fallen pears and even up some broken branches, I realized what a unique tree I had planted. My eyes became focused on the number and size of the pears that were covering a huge area of my yard. I also looked and saw the possibilities of the tree for 2,025.

Before the day was over we had a good supply of fruit put away, the broken limbs were carried off and what was left of the old pear tree stood tall and strong. I realized the weakness had not been in that old pear tree at all. It will grow tall and strong again, and most likely produce more pears, than can be used by one family.

The way I had viewed the circumstance, was the dilemma. It has only been a few short weeks since I almost cut the pear tree down.

Well, I think maybe I'll take a walk, pull a nice ripe pear and rest in the shade of my old pear tree.

Number 88

The rancher shouted, "Open up the gate"
The first herd of cows ran in
And someone yelled
"We're missing number 88"

The cowboys eyed each other
with a sideways grin
When the rancher gave the order
To the new guy, in the pen

"Hey Jake" Go to the east pasture
Bring back 88 and her new calf
The other cowboys got real quiet
Didn't want Jake to hear them laugh

"You won't have any trouble
Just stay on your horse, look her in the eye
Number 88 will come on the double
Won't take you very long, you'll have a real fast ride"

Number 88 and Her New Baby Calf

....

I've heard most all my life, "A Picture is Worth a Thousand Words."
The older I get the more I realize that statement could be correct.
I've heard Photographers say, "You have art, when the person behind the
camera is able to elicit emotion with the picture they have taken."

When I shot this picture of Number 88 and her new baby calf, I was just, simply enjoying
snapping pictures. I understand that from a professional point of view, my picture has
much to be desired. And, with further thought, I can't take any credit as to having a
unique, ability to relay emotional messages to anyone with my picture taking skills.

Although, when the camera is clicked and holds a moment still, it gives me enough time to process.

In this picture, I see another of God's creations. A mother standing guard over her young.
The innocence of the young standing in the shadow and protection of its mother.

That Old Pink Chair

The family's been fed
and the floor has been swept
The bed has been made
No chore has been left

Now that old pink chair
I see over there
Stirs an urge to rest
I can't restrain
That old pink chair
Is calling my name

Don't Send Me Pretty Roses

Don't send me pretty roses
That wouldn't be the same
Let's walk through fields of wild flowers
You gently call my name

Weave those flowers
Through the hair
That's now turned silver gray
Hold my hand and let me know
You love me still today

A Glimpse of Her

. . . .

Today I got a glimpse of her
All colorful and bright
She was beautiful
She shone like gold
In the early morning light

Cool clear waters
Carried her peacefully it seemed
Yes, today I got a glimpse of her
"If life was all downstream"

After I wrote the poem, "A Glimpse of Her", I asked myself,
"Will anyone else know what this poem means?"

I asked several prolific readers to listen and then tell me what the poem meant to them. I got different thoughts from everyone, and all told me they liked the poem. I enjoyed their thoughts, although none of them picked up on my meaning of the poem. Believe it or not, their differing interpretations of the poem, brought me great pleasure. It made me think, more so than before, (Poetry is a thought provoking type of writing.) Maybe it's the rhyme & rhythm that stirs emotions and thoughts?

A Glimpse of Her

In the small town of Lewis, just about everyone knew everyone back in the early 1900's. All of the people were a pretty "Down to Earth" kind of people. Olivia was just a sixteen year old girl then. She was quiet and shy but friendly and helpful, if you know what I mean. She went out of her way to be helpful but did so quietly.

Midsummer, a new family moved to town. They moved into, what was known, in Lewis as, "The Mansion." It was a well known fact that the family moved in from the city and were rich folk. There were three children, twin boys about ten years old and a girl about 16 or so.

In the fall, school began and was filled with students again.
But, the rich folk, didn't send their kids to school. They had a teacher to come to the mansion and teach them there. No one really ever saw much of the people from, the mansion.

Every day, Olivia got up early and helped with chores, before getting ready for school. She helped her mom with inside chores and her dad with outside chores. The family worked hard. Olivia's hands were a little rough and calloused. Her auburn colored hair was thick and shone in the sunlight, but she pulled it back into a pony tail or braided it, most of the time. Sometimes, when she worked outside in the field, her long eyelashes would collect a little dust but her almond colored eyes were still yet bright and inquisitive. She was a happy girl, thankful for all that she and her family had.

Time passed and Olivia heard that the new girl's name was Julia. She thought, "What a pretty name."

By this time she had gotten a glimpse of Julia, a few times; and she always looked beautiful. Olivia thought, "Julia's clothes must have come from New York or wherever fancy clothes come from. She couldn't help compare herself, to Julia.

Needless to say, life went on in the small town of Lewis. Olivia worked hard every day, in school and at home. One hot mid-summer day after the chores were done, Olivia and her mom, went to the creek not far from their cabin. They walked up the path, through the woods and just before they got to the creek, they could hear laughter, ringing out. It was not until they came into the clearing that, Olivia saw Julia in the water. The girl must have been with one of the older women, who worked for Julia's parents.

Julia was graceful and her laughter chimed like the melody of bells. Her skin looked soft and smooth. Her pretty, blond hair was long and silky. She had the prettiest sky blue eyes. When she smiled, her face lit up. She looked calm, peaceful and happy. When she swam, she seemed to float on the water like a golden leaf in the fall; floating downstream in the cool clear water. Although, not unfriendly, the girl and the older woman left the creek and went on their way.

Olivia, gazed wistfully, as Julia disappeared into the thicket. She turned to her mother. "Julia is beautiful. Her hair shines like gold and she seems so peaceful. "Today, I got a glimpse of her. You did too didn't you, Mama?"

Olivia's mother answered. "Today I got a glimpse of her, if life is all downstream."

Days and months went by and then the Depression hit. Life was hard for the rich, the poor and everyone in between. One day Olivia and her mother, got a glimpse of Julia, in town. They had heard that times had not been good for Julia and her family. She carried a small child and held the hand of another. Her hair was a bit unkempt and didn't have quite the shine it had before. Olivia noticed her skin wasn't quite as smooth and the peaceful look in her eyes had changed to one of deep thought and concentration. The kind of look you have when you are trying to make the sort of decision that keeps food on the table.

As Olivia and her mother walked on down the street, Olivia said, "I almost, didn't recognize, Julia."

"You got a glimpse of her today. Life is not all downstream."

Hideaway

I was searching for a hideaway
One pretty autumn day
I slipped on my walking shoes
And I was on my way

To that imaginary place
Where I could toss away my fears
Where my dreams I could sit and chase
And visit childhood years

That Old Wagon

That old wagon out by the barn
Has seen a lot of years
And the old man who drove it
Saw many smiles and tears

In his later days
He told stories of his travelin
When he'd hitch up
Those old ponies to his wagon

He rode in that old wagon
And then he went by car
He watched a rocket on the moon
And saw airplanes among the stars

Now when I look at that old wagon
That's not really what I see
I see my daddy sitting there
His hand upon his knee

I hear the stories of a common man
His laughter and his fears
Yea, when I look at that old wagon
That's not all I see
I can picture Daddy
And what he means to me

She's Always Had My Back

When my appointment day
To get my pup, finally arrived
The flame of my mission
Was rising fast and rising high

She was only eight weeks old
When I took her from her pack
She's been with me
Nine years now
She's always had my back

She's been with me through health issues
Loneliness and fear
She has sat by me for hours
Through laughter and through tears

I am blessed
for when I've needed her
I'd look and she was there
Standing close beside me
Or lying at my feet

She was only eight weeks old
When I took her from her pack
And no matter
How many years she stays
I will always have her back

Waylon and Jessi

She counts them a blessing
Waylon and Jessi
She sees them in the moonlight
Watches as they're dancing

When she whistles
Like a locomotive, they come
She hears hooves hit the ground
Like the beating of a drum

They dance and they prance
They take apples from her hand
They do it very gently
They know she is a friend

Waylon and Jessi

She whispers their names
As she strokes their pretty heads
Yes, she counts them as a blessing
Waylon and Jessi

But when they've stayed a while
She lets them take their flight
Then she watches from a distance
Deep into the night

She counts them as a blessing
Waylon and Jessi
She sees them in the moonlight
And watches, as they're dancing

Blossoms in the Sky

....

When we all get tangled up in life
And everyday beauty isn't clear
Maybe we should take a breath
Look another way
And let a different picture appear

"I looked up and saw
Blossoms in the Sky"
"What I see is the way I look"

Mr. Robin Redbreast

. . . .

Mr. Robin Redbreast
I saw you there, today
You were sitting on my window sill
And then you flew away

I still can hear your pretty song
Floating in the breeze
Are you saying, Robin Redbreast
You're bringing in the Spring

At First Glance

. . . .

At first glance, I saw the cloud
And thought my little world was covered in ice
I looked again
And saw the beauty of the horizon begin

I told myself, "Don't be so quickly deceived"
Always take time
To stop, look and listen
For what you really believe

Please join me
on Facebook

Sharon J. Millican

Other names I use for my books
Sharon J. Beard
Sharon J. Sockey

Thank you to all my readers

Sharon J. Millican

Sharon J. Millican

Text 4798062574 & let me know what you think of the book—
Thanks to my readers!

Sharon J. Millican (Pettigrew) has also written books under the names of:

Sharon J. Sockey: (Like a Panther in the Night)
& (Down by the Barn): <u>A Book of Pictures and Poetry</u>

Sharon J. Beard: (Koke Goes to Oklahoma) & (Raven Goes to Arkansas)

Sharon J. Millican: (Why I Call Her Friend) & (What I Found When
I Wasn't Looking): <u>A Book of Pictures, Poetry and Prose</u>

Printed in the United States
by Baker & Taylor Publisher Services

What I Found When I Wasn't Looking is a book of Pictures, Poetry and Prose. These are writings open to interpretation of the individual. Filled with simple writings; it may bring laughter or tears and allow the reader to reminisce and think.

Sharon J. Millican (Pettigrew) is author of the Recently, published books: Why I Call Her Friend & What I Found When I Wasn't Looking. She has also written books under the names: Sharon J. Sockey and Sharon J. Beard. Sharon also enjoys songwriting and photography. She lives in Oklahoma, and is currently working on her next book.

U.S. $18.99

ISBN 979-8-3850-3251-8

5 1 8

WESTBOW
PRESS®
A DIVISION OF THOMAS NELSON
& ZONDERVAN

9 798385 032518